ALL NATURE IS A SACRAMENTAL FIRE

To my lively, bouncy, creative, and
much-loved granddaughter Emily.

In gratitude to the Pittsburgh Foundation – and to the
Joseph Calihan family – for a grant that enabled Eliz-
abeth Shaw to put these verses together and edit them.

Other Titles of Interest from St. Augustine's Press

Joseph Bottum, *The Second Spring*

Joseph Bottum, *The Fall and Other Poems*

Ralph McInerny, *The Soul of Wit: Some Poems*

Ralph McInerny, *Shakespearean Variations*

Catherine O'Neil & Zbigniew Janowski, *Juliusz Słowacki's
'Agamemnon's Tomb'*

Michael Davis, *The Poetry of Philosophy*

Marion Montgomery, *With Walker Percy at the Tupperware Party:
In Company with Flannery O'Connor, T.S. Eliot, and Others*

ALL NATURE IS
A SACRAMENTAL FIRE
MOMENTS OF BEAUTY, SORROW, AND JOY

MICHAEL NOVAK

St. Augustine's Press
South Bend, Indiana

Manufactured in the United States of America

1 2 3 4 5 6   16 15 14 13 12 11

Library of Congress Cataloging in Publication Data
Novak, Michael.
All nature is a sacramental fire:
moments of beauty, sorrow, and joy / Michael Novak.
p. cm.
ISBN 978-1-58731-022-5 (paperbound: alk. paper)
I. Title.
PS3564.O9A79 2011
811'.54 – dc22   2011010063

∞ The paper used in this publication meets the minimum require-
ments of the American National Standard for Information Sciences –
Permanence of Paper for Printed Materials, ANSI Z39.48-1984.

ST. AUGUSTINE'S PRESS
www.staugustine.net

CONTENTS

PIECES FROM THE FLAMES
Through My Friends, the Senses

The Lord God Creator has given us five openings to the physical world around us, that sacramental world in which we swim: hearing, sight, taste, touch, and smell. The experience of each of these senses is sometimes sharp and clean; poignant, evocative, almost unendurable. In these few lines below, penned during sixty years, I have tried to snatch from the flames of rushing time a few simple pieces, shards, remainders. "All Nature is a Heraclitean Fire," a real poet wrote. I am but an amateur. But one who believes, however, that everybody should write poetry, or reach for it. It is the language of our soul. It is concentrated prose.

A poet? I truly miss being one. Instead, I have welcomed joy into my life by being as open to, aware of, my five senses as I can. When the power of their beauty overwhelms me, there is also joy in pressing the sweet from it as succinctly as I can, in words.

I've never learned the discipline of meter, scansion, rhyme. Nor have the basics of composing poetry been taught me by a poet. The poor best I can do is pull from memory fragments I have read or heard – bursts of music or color, texture, unusual words that wrapped around them, melodies that stirred my mind.

It was great fun to try and capture connected bursts of physical experiences in just a line or two. It rinsed my soul to do so. And so, to bring more joy into my life, I often picked up pen and paper, and began to write in prose as concentrated and musical as I could possibly achieve. These fragments are derivative and borrowed. But they did bring joy to me.

The sharpest impressions were made on me by friends. And so on holidays or anniversaries, or other days of celebration, I felt sometimes much moved to render feelings for that other, in words more formal, more compressed, more taut, than ordinary speech.

Sometimes I wrote these lyrics in a notebook, more often on scraps of paper from which I later copied them. Sometimes lines appeared to me while dozing, and I would waken long enough to put them down, before the music fled. (Do not neglect the humblest modes of inspiration. Close your fists around them quickly while in your grasp, seize them in mid-flight. They evanesce into the night.)

Beauties resist capture, desperately so at times. In the mind they come so vivid, only to slip away as morning mist. They gave me wrestling matches. They refused to bend. Visions disappear. One must arise and fell them with the swiftest arrows in one's stock. Or they will be whisked away.

Sharp, clean tastes of life are not always available to us. We are busy. We seldom notice.

Therefore, I formed the habit of opening myself to sensory experiences all day long. Letting them enter through my freedom, through my senses, through the sacramental sheen by which the world of our Creation shows itself to me – overpowers me.

Down the years, reading back through these poor pages has reminded me of passing beauty; has often given pleasure; and bade me break from the routines I had been falling into, to observe the world around me (pouring into me) more keenly. Beauties took me by the shoulder, punched my ribs, whispering: "Notice me. Don't be so busy. Stop and smell the autumn leaves, the sparks from fires at the curb, the acrid falling of the spring and summer into winter death. It is so beautiful. It is so fleeting. Capture it!"

The Narrative

A few words about the story of my life after 1953, when I was twenty, and these poems begin, to help the reader grasp the pieces I was snatching from the flames. I had decided early, against my parents' wishes, to begin studying for the priesthood just before I turned fourteen, at Notre Dame du Lac in Indiana – where sits the famous University. After that, a year of novitiate in North

Dartmouth, Massachusetts, the town next over from New Bedford where *Moby Dick* begins.

The first verses collected here arose at Stonehill College, some forty miles due north, where I was sent to study as a newly professed religious of the Congregation of Holy Cross. It was there that an early verse of mine won the poetry prize from the New England Association of Catholic Colleges, and was chosen as the verse for the inside cover of our college yearbook. I was just completing freshman year. Stonehill's campus is one of the most beautiful I know, and there the beauty of the fields, the lake, the birds, the sounds of crows and hawks, burned into me. A number of these lyrics come from there. And it was there I read Maritain's *Creative Intuition in Art and Poetry* – it was so beautiful I had to leave my desk, go outside, and walk down to the lake.

After graduation, the Congregation assigned me to Rome for further study. My God, the stimulation! But most of all, I admired my friends – Dave Burrell, Nick Ayo, Jim Burtchaell, John Dunne, Harry Baker, Jim Simonson, and many others – golly! were they smart and lively, good-looking, serious, generous, good fun. I fell in love with Rome, the palpable everything about it.

Yet inner turmoil would not leave me. I loved the priesthood, I looked forward to it, and yet I dreaded it, it did not seem right, I was confused. After two years of torment – torment of beauty, torment of lack of peace – a wise superior called me back to the United States. "Do not make such a decision abroad. Make it in your own country. Otherwise you will long regret it." He assigned me to Washington, where with splendid counsel from the most inspired spiritual director I have ever known, a genial saint, and from a most kind and brilliant psychoanalyst, it came clear to me, and all, that God called me elsewhere.

So on January 1, 1960, I began a new life. I left my happy studies for the priesthood – very lucky was I, to gain such an education, as much through the torments of the final years as from the books I dearly loved. With a hundred dollars from my father, and a partially completed novel, I left for New York City, determined not to take a job but only write. I found a garret in the upper Bronx, across the street from Fordham. I dated lots of girls, even lost my heart twice.

4

But I did complete the novel, and sold it to Doubleday in June. Somehow, through a high school friend, I wrote speeches for an aspiring congressman from New Jersey, and sent one (on "the New Frontier") to the campaign of John F. Kennedy, before his inauguration. Archibald Cox wrote with thanks, and encouraged me to keep sending things.

Harvard and Yale each offered me a fellowship to study philosophy. I chose Harvard, because it gave a little more money – and I needed every cent. At Harvard, I fell in love again with a very secular, kind girl, then several others, and I was dating three wonderful women when I was invited on a blind date with a girl from Iowa in March of 1962. Her name was Karen, and in five minutes I knew that I would marry her. It took a year for me to persuade her to become engaged to me. At last, then, she was happy with her ring, and what it meant about the two of us. She had certainly fled away from me again and again, and I had to be constant and persistent until, like a courageous bluefish on a line, she tired out. She ran out of arguments for 'No', is the way she put it.

We took our honeymoon in Rome, at the second session of Vatican Council II. Not long after, I was offered a position at Stanford University, then SUNY Old Westbury, then a chair at Syracuse, and finally a chair in 1978 at the American Enterprise Institute, the leading private 'think tank' in the world.

Karen became an accomplished – no, a great – painter and printmaker, sculptor, too, in bronze. (Her work may be seen at www.laub-novakart.com.) She insisted on her independence and her separate space from start to finish. She was the strongest, most independent, and yet warmest, sweetest woman God ever made, and he entrusted her to me for forty-six years, until her death in 2009, when she was just short of 72. The last verses in this book are for her.

This is the slender narrative from which these pieces from the flames were snatched. I wish that I had truly been a poet, not an amateur, to capture them more beautifully, so that they might be worthy of the Creator from Whose sweet hands they came. I did my best.

STONEHILL

(1952-1956)

Undergraduate Days
Professed Religious
of the
Congregation of
Holy Cross

෩1෪

The Meteorite

Crickets chirping;
Dewed grass at finger's touch;
Night skies that
Soothe one's eyes
And silhouetted pines
Play ogres, warriors,
In disguise.

Summer skies!
Dark, pure, and infinite.
Silver sparks and gold
Straining to lay hold
our earth –

When reddened ember flows
Oh! So slow
across a nearby arc of sky.
(Yet lingers where
it broke from someone's care
and shouted there –
from Paradise.)

⚅2⚇

Life is alone
Like crow's caw
     over frosted field
Like footfalls
     on a gravel path
Like one cloud in huge blue sky
Like a teen-age girl
     with child
Like a sea gull wheeling in the air
A firefly in the dark yard
An old man
     caught in the rain
A stone's plunk
     deep in a well
Like a jet's drone
     shocking the sky.

Ocean floor never quite seen
Wind's sound never yet caught
Dark path never yet trod
Life is alone.

1953

⬥3⬥

Don't Make a Nuisance of Yourself

Once, before my recent
Evolution,
I made a grave and serious
Resolution.
I SWORE
With masculinity and puissance:
"Be damned
Before
You e'er become a nuisance!"

Now, my Darwinian
evolution
has seen improvement on that
resolution.
By my determination's awful puissance
I'm now a damned (and simultaneous) nuisance!

1953

୧୫4୨୦

Looking Upwards on the Seacoast

Brittle sunlight splintered on the street.
I saw a stucco building paled to mauve,
    A yellow turned to buff.

I saw a bell hung in the sky.
(The cold air clanged up there,
    And stung my face.)

How close the sky is to the Earth.

                                    1953

C/3580

Cousin Fran

I love the quiet of her way
I love to hear her softly say:
"You did?"
I love the wonder in her eyes
Her dress the color of the bluest skies.
I love the lilt of kindness in her voice,
Her silent laugh that makes the sea rejoice
I love the fire leaping in her breast
Of restlessness and other-promised rest.

A voyage silent as a ship at sea
So joyful seems Keith's fiancée to me.

1953

ଓଓ6ଓଓ

Our Lady of Stonehill

Flung!
Flakes whirl, swirl
    in the silence, whispering, fall.
Cars creep through the hall
Of the trees.

Moccasins climbed once the low hill
    (now hooded in stillness and snowfall).
Through leaf lace of May
Indians saw, silent, the heights of wind-silvered blue.
Octobers, the settler looked over the rust grass, over
    the gold light, spilling over the swells of his
    fields.
Along here, of summer, riches have cantered,
    riding down bridal paths bending with sun.

And now look!
Here – in the dark, scented fir
Here – in the old coppered oak
Here – on the grey weathered hill.
(In the snow-fall; in the leaf-fire; in the sun-splash)
Wearing the seasons, She stands here
    Blessing them all.

Strong is her grotto, and hard:
Made of earth-stones.
One joined together with one:
All of them (all of us) one.

With all men that were, and will be,
With snow weaving a forest
With trees full of spring's fragrance,
With autos, and car-whine, and wires bright
      in the sun:

"We are the stones of thy grotto!
Mary! We are thy Christ
Come
Be in midst of us
Mary, oh! mother us
(the ages of Earth of us):
Christ!"

1954

*This verse was awarded the New England Association of Catholic Colleges prize for poetry in 1954.

ᘓ7᙭

Mary! Thou hast Christ fleshed
Nine mother-months Him flushed:
And if Head, body; Vine, shoots; Shrine, stones.
Thou stand'st white 'midst His stones
Thou art millions' His mother.

We are – Mary mother – shrine's stones
We are – Mary mother – Christs
Come!
Stand in the midst of us
Mary, oh! mother us
Christs.

1954

ℭ𝔤8𝔟ℭ

The Blessed Virgin Mary & the Moon

The milk-white moon outspreads its raiment in the skies
    And veils the quiet stars with finest weave.
        Or, age-warm coin it is, worth-buying coin: oh,
    thieve
This silver, use, and spend: life's hour flies.

See how she pales the dark night's purple dyes?
        See how the glinting pines are silent in the eve?
        See how the earth is motionless and moon-won?
Leave thy cares:
Her love doth silver thee and skies.

The night breeze sweeps the leaves against the sky
    And, silvered so, they whisper. Someone sighs
So soft: "For what this silver but to buy?
        And Christ – my Son – a purchase is and prize!
Leave not my silver-worth unspent on high –
        But spend it, spend, O! Spend beneath the skies!"

1954

15

ভ৯ৎ

On Loving Chaucer

When that autumn and her breezes cool
The lovely leaves on stiffened branches pull
To float them, yellow, turning, robin-breasts
Against the free blue sky; when sunlight rests
Her gentle warmth upon the full-clothed limbs
Of fire in the trees: flaming bronze and red
And yellow leaping in the breeze against
The air-blue, rainwashed, scented sky; while fenced-
In self looks, longs, to bolt and play
Amongst infinities of space, and bird-wing
Into God: then school begins to ring
Self down with iron duties, rake and splay
With tasks – yet strangest paradox! That there
My spirit basks.

1954

ೲ10ೲ

Spring is Long

My hands throb: look! The life in them
Yes, yes! The life, the bending of them
I hear the pounding heart, the blood, the ever-flowing
Warmth, the human things:
Digestion's growl, a swallow, breathings
In the nose. I see the all-blue skies, clouds going
Crazily and dancing white-green leaves
Above my head. I hear the phoebe whistle
Joyously upon a bobbing purple thistle
In the sunshine-swinging grass: Nothing grieves
No, nothing in the wide blue green and swimming
Living world can grieve me though I am and then
Am not. Spring is long. Two thousand springs
Are infinite compared to me: how men –
How many men – like me, do live from life:
That life then millions long, enduring, oaken
Strong. From It I am, I am, I am
I AM! and then am gone. Too swift, you think?
I stammer how to say it is not swift
But all-cupped-up-in-hands eternal drink!

1956

ઉ૩11ૹૐ

Reflections on Tire Treads

"Soft mud gushes.
Oh. You know."
"Soft mud rushes
Then falls slow;

Spills as waves spill –"
" – look! you see –"
" – then holds still
So actively!"

Mud was formless,
Meaningless,
Begging, somehow.
Tire's stress.

Now I read it
joyously!
Maybe God will
Drive through me!

1956

ଔ12ଓ

Jesu Dulcis Memoria (A Translation)

Jesu, dulcis memoria,
dans vera cordis gaudia:
sed super mel et omnia
ejus dulcis praesentia.

Nil canitur suavius,
nil auditur jucundius,
nil cogitatur dulcius,
quam Jesus Dei Filius.

– St. Bernard of Clairvaux

———

Sweet is mere memory of Him
Coursing through the heart with joy
And sweeter far than honeyed bread
His presence is. How sweet.

No hymn more gentle-sweet
No chord more jubilant
No thought more piercing sweet
Than Jesus Son of God.

1956

Cೞ13ಹ

I

The mist is thick tonight out on the sea.
Rolling, swirling dusk has caught
Me all alone.
I am unsteady, sick, up, down and not
A moment still.
Always, always waste is all
And loneliness.
Empty, empty water craving dawn.

II

How high? How far can eyes
    Pore? In purity, streams of – oh! without-end – skies?
    Search, stretch, strive for the height of, strain for the glaze
Of, the glisten all wind-whirléd blue of the cold-heighted
    haze!

Cool, sucking, shadow-depthed water below:
    Tense, lapping, light-angles flashing to reach –
    Flowing, unfolding, yearning for infinite air
And the whipped whited clouds, out! up where the sun sings!

Dazzle light! Sky, water, rise of the sun!
Bright wetness on grass; whispers of wavy white leaves
The scent, shadow, leaving of pines; the fall of a leaf;
A silveréd web; leaves streamed-through with sun;
The web-needled bank; birds rinsing the air with their song!
Winds cleansing the earth, make my morn dawn!

1956

ᑫ14ᒣ

Thy love is April twilight
There is no sound
But crickets chirping
The pines that rise above the silent water
Gesture at the dark.

My steps
Crack needles of the pines
Two ducks hustle
From the perfect stillness into
distant dusk.

The green-streaked pines scream
back at me: Life is a waste
You are alone
But dusk is over everything
and still.

1956

ROME
(1956–1958)

Soon after my arrival in Rome, the Hungarian
Revolution rolled the surface of the earth. Eastern
Europe moved closer to us. My destinies as Amer-
ican and Slav drew near. For two years I studied
theology, took courses from Bernard Lonergan,
s.j., and visited every part of Italy I could get to.
These were two of the happiest years of my life.

And in

WASHINGTON, D.C.
(August 1958–January 1960)

The darkest and most difficult days of my life,
when I was trying to discern whether or not God
willed me to depart from the blessed path to ordi-
nation. Those bleak days, as these verses testify,
were also laced with joy and love, as the dark
nights often are.

❧15❧

Budapest, November 4, 1956

My people, my people, what have they done to thee?
Saith Christ. Ugly concrete, ugly ugly streets
Where flags where people wave where tanks
Like unsquashed beetles move and grate
And boom. Where dirt and stone and plaster
Fall. It is so many years, so many years
And is it all in vain? My people, why?
Thy children run to death with bottle-bombs
They fight from fallen bricks with no place left
To run, from ancient dirty broken bricks
How can you die
Forgetful of your wives, your boys, your little
girls: where are they now, my people, where?
And you my daughters, you without your sons,
Your husbands, fathers, you must wait against
The damp cemented cellars, in crash and
fire-roar and choking dust, and wait for death
– for you or them.
In so few days from peace and table
Now to death, in stone cold streets away.
        Or now, perhaps, November sixth, already
Dead: The press-releases frozen false, the swaying
arm now stiff, a living shout now still,
As men now sway from silent lamp posts in the street.

No one, no one comes to aid, but death
And dying on the dirt, the pavements, stones,
uptorn and shocked and cold.

23

My people, O! my people.
They will carry you away
Out of the past and home and love
Into a land of stone,
Despair and loneliness your bread
Now endlessly for years and years
My people, oh!
        And those who stand in
Armored tanks with turtle-plated coats?
O God! of them? What has become
Of them? How can it be, how can it be
That they can look on people, bodies,
People, shoot and shoot and kill?
That they should use incendiary bombs
Until my people burn and run,
Out in the open shot or twisted,
Hanged, how can it be? My Father,
Yes, if I must drink, must drink it,
Yes.

So must men do. It is the logic of
Their lives. They do and do and ever on,
My Father, always, always on. A nation
Dies, ten thousands scream in pain
And loves are separated in the dark and cold.
My Father, yes. Their will be done.
They will not change. On You, my Father,
You it will be blamed. How can a good. . . ?
In view of, view of . . . Be their will done.
They can, they can, without compassion,
Live apart from love, draw mechanic laws
That murder men, commands that slay.
My Father! Love beyond life, making
Roots, growth, warmth,

Seas both blue and breakered, skies and
Hearts, My Father, Love! – Man
Lives without Thee,
So, world without, years and years,
against me; be His will, people,
O! my long, long people, done.

December 1956

ೞ16ಜಾ

Gianiculum in Spring

Rome is now like blossoms in the sky
Like clouds against a silver sky
Like mountains violet and white
Off in the pale, pale evening sky.

Like roof-tops centuries old
And sun

Like infants' wobbly legs
And mothers' eyes

Like scarves and kerchiefs, smiles
And hearts

Like meditations in an old man's
Mind, as he looks over Rome
From Garibaldi's park, in spring.

1957

Smiles at Witnessing Success

Gladness sprang about the bus, rang every
Glass and face and coat and song from
All mankind: man can be glad!
Man can be glad! His history, suffering
Smiles because today in all these crowds
Of people standing in the bus a child
Of two did smile a smile of love
As mother laughing reached her to the overhanging
Bar to clutch – of love and joy and infinite success!

1957

❦18❧

To Joan of Arc, In Italy

There! Beyond the stucco rimming round my sight
The Earth: Whole roll of blue – or is it – hills
And off beyond, is what? Is what a vast
Untold-of multitude of souls on seas and hills,
Even in these booted miles of land.
Within this rim how many loves? Or sorrows,
Aches and tears? Or rooms of what delight,
Or childish love or blinds drawn dark?
Or dirt and suffering behind the walls,
Or lusts and angers, griefs and laughs? – All is,
It is all here, unseen. I am in pain
Because I cannot see, nor love. Who?
Oh, who can brim so vast a cup of love?

There is one. It is *He* – but He is dead.
And though He drinks and offers round
The centuries do not drink.
And Joan (and I) cry pain.

Inside, most horrible complacence –
When, the windows opening, burst in the out-
Side air with fields and trees and Alpine hills
And snow: a purple filled my eyes,
Kaleidoscoped wheat's yellow like a flare.
And blue sky flipped eternally away
Without an end or word or sign.
Then rolling clouds broke back to finitude
And slipped a sunlit glorious word uncannily

Into my lungs like knives of freshening
air, the brilliant battle-light of Alps
And valleys in the night's despair.

Summer 1957

⳽1980

The Bubble

Our friendship reflected like silver the sun
And rainbowed a circle-bright square
Until you consistently mocked me
And blocked me –
And popped it to nothing but air.

1957

∝20≈

Mirror Sketches of
Two Mutually Reflecting Friends

The rain falls soft tonight; outside, the asphalt
Glistens. The Lord has finished Benediction.
My friends and I are soon to bed.
I have thought a poem-round of all
To honor them, and God, and aid our
Charity. For God is love and they designs
Of His. Their lives write out his thoughts,
Their bents bend from His breath, their eyes
Steal light from His.

Dave Burrell

Is a spiral-flame of fire
In the night. Not many times
Has man scorned body, time,
Mechanic needs as he –
He is all soul. His will
Grasps on a thing: no one
Will halt him short.
He questions, asks, intent –
His mind is thirst or flame
And all his days consumed.
He prays with seriousness –
His muscles stiff and
Uncoordinate in games.
Just as he leans his head
In prayer and fiercely closes eyes
Just so, his heart rebukes stiff failing

Efforts of his hands to catch
A ball. To Dave, all things
Are 'challenging,' all people
'wonderful,' events 'exciting':
Everything is dancing light on Plato's wall
Of blue-skied open brilliant
Flame Beyond – whereto he runs,
Toward which he spirals, flickering.

Nick Ayo

Has read the dictionary
Slept ungainly times with gain
And otherwise
Does quite as he decides.
A most unusual chap
He'll laugh and clap
His hands upon his knees
As likeably as Puck,
As at his ease.
Opinion passes him
Without a stop
And should
He think to climb a tree
He would – unless at sea
Or other treeless place.
He bears a grace
Of manner that is
All Nick's own – his
Fork he lifts to lips
As mildly as sun slips
Into the day; and he
Would soon as not
Let go an argument
Than catch or caught

32

Be on some battlement
Of hairs. Yet curiosity
Lights up his pale green eye
And softest tone
Of his may but belie
A thrust aimed at your bone
With searching point –
Your sureness to disjoint.
He'll give no rest
But like the Grecian gnat –
This by no means jest –
Will query
'Why?'
No matter where in argument you're at
And with most massive
Innocence of eye.
He's not so passive
As he looks –
Nor could he be
With so much joy in books
And life he wants to see!

1957

∞21∞

Venice

What man can do
Is seen in what he's done
What man has done
Is best enjoyed
When it has gone.
So Venice meets the heart
(The heart, not mind, for Venice
Is not Florence, is not Rome.)

Venice is water
Blue in brilliant sun
Like lightning in the sun,
Or grey like colored mirrors of lead.
Venice
Is the purples
And flesh-tints
Of paintings:
Rooms on rooms
Of Tintoretto and Tiziano.

Venice is a sweet romance
A quiet beauty, very thin –
That is how you know it is romance.

Venice is for visits
And for dreams.

Waters woo the heart
Into their silvered web:
The sun falls on the palaces
And gothic lace,
And painted pilings,
And little archéd bridges
Lie in dark.

Gondoliers are happy
They are real
Their shirts are white
And their straw hats
Red ribbons
Still in one's heart
On faraway
And shimmering sea.

Venice is also St. Mark's –
Gold, serene, its orchestra
At play, the fluttering
Wings of two thousand pigeons:
Symbols of grace?
Somebody's sign?
Numerous as people,
Domestic, fluttering, kind.

Ice cream, then, at dusk
Or coffee, wine,
And ever the music:
Thousands of people
Underneath the moon
On the góndola-broken
Lagoon.

Quiet, so quiet, Venice
Even the singers
At night in the lighted
Violet fleet
Only sweeten the night,
And the stillness of the
Water, the still lapping
Of the water, in the cool
Of night.

1957

⊗22⊗

In Praise of Cousin Fran and God

Where is woman more to me than you?
Or joy more girl-like meeting motherhood? Or
O! Miracle! That from you, child, now three –
Michael, Bette Ann, and Keith – are
Living, large, all
But electric-charged with life
For ages hence: from you! From that heart
That I love, that mind – as if by fingers
Life-caressed and formed: received and steeped
In ocean-riches of your days: of patience,
Quietness, restraint, and love,
Of devilment and coquetry of – oh!
I cannot say, I cannot say what is the
Mystery God's placed in you
          (But be He praised!)
And let thy children grow as oaks sprung
          from thy soil!

1957 and 1961

ৎ৪23৮ও

Frater et in Christo Es, Dear Dick.

Loyalty, Dick, is your name
And I love it – loyalty.
Since we were kids.
Do you remember the boat that you bought me,
Metal, propellored, yellow-blue,
Bought for more than you had for your gifts
And hid for joy of surprise –
Till it fell with a clank from its wrap
And loud as your heart in despair?
Hopeless I was to live up to your love
Hopeless am I even now.

Brothers be we for a few short years
Brothers before we go. A moment's
Joy and love until – swift from the wrap
The yellow boat falls through our fingers
Before we can catch it, shatters the silence
Of love. Or, wait! Is it froze in the air?
like memory there of your boat, and He-is
and we-are, and ever shall be,
Brotherly: we.

1959

❧24❧

For Sister Madaleva

Mary, Magdalen, and Eve –
Or simply, woman.
Wife of God,
Her life was to conceive
A thousand loves.

The long blue sea was not so restless
As her heart,
The canyon not so deep, nor silent
As her loneliness.

She is God's wife
It is their jubilee:
The pangs are over with
Her loves will never be!

1959

⊰25⊱

One Step Toward Tolerance

Is that Jones anticlerical!
He'll never see a priest
Without he'll curse and swear at him
Beneath his breath, at least.

Now, nothing like the priesthood
Holds back our progress-pace
And nothing like religion
Is the bugbear of the race.

I too am anticlerical
But dignified and mild –
To men *I* cannot tolerate
At least I've always smiled.

1959

ೞ26ೲ

The Casuists

Arguments of casuistry
Can be a lot of fun
Not because they're challenging –
Because they're never done.

You argue and you argue
To make a case concrete,
Till the rising flood of details
Climbs up above your feet.

No philosophic import,
Or course, confounds the case
Facts solely are the issue.
They stare you in the face.

And yet the strangest thing
Of all lies hidden in a fact:
Although discussion's most concrete
The rules are still abstract.

1959

⚙27⚙

The Lotus

Lotus blossom
Floating on the water
Mirror, carnival
Of color: peace.

1959

ぼ28හ

Autumn, 1959

Maple top
Against the blue
Flaming orange and gold
Heroic: soon to die.

⊂இ29ഇ⊃

Wintry Air

Breath is cold
In piercing bluest
Wintry air: the sky
Has entered human lungs.

1959

≪30≫

Winter's Trees

Winter's trees
Stand straight, in black
And greying remnant
Leaves, beneath the rain.

1959

ଓଃ31ଃ୦

The Lord

The Lord
Like love is huge
Great canyons deep, majestic,
And lovely as a baby's smile.

1959

‹§32›

The Lady

O Lady
Queen, I love you not
As queen, as mother
Surely do.

1959

CB33BO

The Canticle

Woman's breasts
As lovely does
Do, leap from sunshine
Into forest dark.

1959

○♥34♣○

Trees Afire
(Memories of October in New England)

Trees afire
With such splendid fire
As the sun – or clouds
Resplendent as the air, as gleaming
Shining knives, desire!
Trees of fire,
Tongues of red and yellow,
Sparkling bronzes heave
To heat the paling sky;
Or scream a drunken
Colored revel back to God.

1959

The Two Freedoms

Birth control and thought control
Throw gears in creaking strife:
Utopian mechanics
Grinding up contingent life!

Censorized or insulized
Life isn't really free,
But thoughts and loves
Are everywhere run through machinery.

Children five, ye gads alive!
Majorities would stop,
Yet scorn the while minorities
For tight'ning freedom's top.

Birth control and thought control:
Imagination's doom.
They kill the mind and ruin love
Until the final boom!

Who now depends on nature's ends
With unmechanic clasp?
Where are men who take their risks
Both freedoms in their grasp?

1959

ೞ36ೲ

Magic too Moves Mountains (The Housekeeper)

A lady once I knew
Was some little like a shrew
Yet holy, by golly!
She knew
Her wrathfulness she should eschew.

Her temper raged at the priests
On both ferials and feasts
And when mad, egad!
The priests
You would think had been beasts.

She prayed, this lady, 'O Lord!'
And most of the saints she quite bored
For often to soften
The Lord
She piously wore the green cord.

Some good, she hoped, it might do her,
The bright little greenish scapular,
But still high, oh my!
Flew her voice to the sky
If a curate but opened his trap to her.

One curate – the worst of all –
Caused the lady a terrible fall.
One day: "Away!"
His call
Found her at his door in the hall.

Her fury knew no bounds
(As awesome as all of this sounds)
But she swore and tore
"O zounds!"
(And worse) in her wrath on her rounds.

But then she thought it through
Prayerfully saw what to do
'Neath his rug very snug
She grue-
Somely planted the scapular true.

A lady once I knew
Some little bit of a shrew –
It worked! He was jerked
From the blue
By the bishop, with little to-do.

1959

ᏕᏗ37ᏇᎧ

I Love To Be Out Walking in the Spring

I love to be out walking in the spring
I love to hear the jays and sparrows sing
I love to feel the sun warm up the earth
And listen while the jonquils come to birth.

Why is it that I love to walk in spring?
What is it makes the bluebirds thrill to sing?
Where does the sun warm up before it warms
The tulips in its tender arms?

I love to be out walking in the spring
I love to hear the jays and sparrows sing
I love to feel the sun rest on the earth
And listen while the jonquils come to birth.

Who knows (not I) the breeze's path in spring?
What makes the cold clean air begin to ring,
When grass has told the tree, and tree the sky
It's time the whole wide world to vivify?

All I know is how I love the spring
Love the wood where birds begin to sing
Love to feel the winds in boisterous play
Love the scents that tulips lend the day.

1959

❧38❧

God's Sweet Goodness Gave to Me

How I love the distance from the sea
That God's sweet goodness gave to me:
Respite, rest, oasis of the years,
A closeness to Himself
No fears of Him, nor frights, nor awkwardness
But blessed foretaste of His tenderness.
Dear God, my dear, with what
Shall I repay this blissful everlasting day?

1959

CR39BO

Ilka at Seventeen

I remember the green green grass
The wet green grass on my feet
And the white trees and the apples
And the sun
And the pines dripping the rain of the night
And oh! the great blue sky
And the valley of Brixen
"When (she said) I was seventeen
And happy
And I loved:
      Loved seventeen and the sky and the trees
      – And owned the sun as I loved!"

1958

MANHATTAN

(January–August 1960)

Afer reaching the profound decision that God did not call me to become a priest – not after all this, not after all these years – I did the typical writerly thing. I packed my bags for New York City, to crash into the big world as a small-town boy from western Pennsylvania mining country. A novel came of it: *The Tiber Was Silver* (1961).

⋘40⋙

Where Is the Girl Who Will Be Wife to Me

Who is my love whom I have yet to see?
Where is the girl who will be wife to me?
She's short? Or slim? Or blond? Or black-
Haired as the Ethiope? The columned ivory
Of the Song, her breasts as drops of myrrh?
The deer leap through the woods in shadowed light
My dear has made no exit from the night.

1960

∞41∞

Imagining

There is sunshine on the sand and rolling
Waves. And you, my wife, my children climbing
On my knee; my books and music; sunsets
I have seen bring silence to the earth;
Bring stars on winter nights. My Lord, my love,
How empty is a life where You are not?

1960

ೞ42ೞ

Ride Silent in the Car

What is there, lady, I can say to you?
You know what passes in my heart, you hear
The meaning of the words unsaid, you sense the love
I do not speak about. The time will come.
For now a kiss upon the lips is all
we'll say, ride silent in the car
awaiting day.

1960

ଓ୫43ୄ

Farewell, My Love

Woman, I loved you
In a way I can't explain
I'm sorry to leave you
(for a while it gave me pain).
I wanted you happy
And liked your voice and liveliness.
The sorrow of your heart
I wanted you happy
But instead the Lord said: part.

The Lord said? No, you said.
It comes out to the same.
The fact is, we're parting
In Him, I'll rest the blame.
Still I do love you
For His, and not my, aim.

Spring 1960

○§44§○

New York City in the Night

The city sky is warm with fog
And it is raining in the streets
The sky is violet tonight and rose
The air is sweet

The windows of the buildings show a warmth tonight
The buildings tower in the colored fog.
The autos splash the mirrors in the street tonight
The men and women really seem to smile.

A young boy made another scream tonight
A young man made his lover shy
A mother laughed with boisterous noise tonight
I think I heard a mother cry.

The light hung soft about New York tonight
The fog made all the men as one
The violet and rose illuminated men tonight
The city, city shone beneath the fog.

July 1, 1960

❧45❧

For three hundred years
Movement occurred
On the quiet island of Manhattan
The sky endured
(Though nobody noticed)
Winds blew
The mists arose from the sea
Millions stirred
Year in and year out
Died and were born
The mists blew in from the sea.

The dust arose in the park,
One night.
The wind blew in from the sea
It whispered a word in the trees
That long, long night
As it used to do
Before the movement on Manhattan.
The wind blew in from the sea
To seize a moment of silence
As in the old time
On the island of Manhattan.

July 3, 1960

❀46❀

As I Saw What the Lord Could Do

The sycamores laughed in the flashing sun
And sawed at the silver blue
The ocean leapt at the wind's command
In grey, and silver, and green
Colors danced in the waters in boats
Where the waters slid and turned.
The clouds were high like a silent sea
Stroked on the distant sky.
We tossed and bounced and felt the spray
We filled our eyes with the sea.
I wondered as I saw what the Lord can do
Why He's done all this for me.

July 4, 1960

HARVARD

(1960–1965)

Harvard offered me a larger grant than Yale did for a Ph.D. scholarship. Having nothing in the bank, for me that was decisive. What I would live on beyond room and tuition, I did not know. It turned out to be writing and lecturing, plus a timely Kent Fellowship.

෴47෴

Why are you quiet,
Like a Sphinx reserved?
Quite willing, surely, if I ask you for a kiss,
Quite kindly bending as becomes a loving miss –
Yet serving not, but only being served?

Do you play games with me?
Or have you dreamed a little test
To heat desire to its best?
What am I supposed to do
– Or be?

1960

∞48∞

The coals are red.
The flames leap in my mind
Still orange, and thin, and swift.
The fire turns to ash.

I love you, dear.
Your lips so still,
Your lips pressed onto mine,
We are at rest.
The earth spins on
Relentlessly –

We have loved
And wrung a moment free.

November 1960

⚜49⚜

Nostra Pace

Our lives are like the smoke of fires
Like the flame
That disappears.
We do not know the reasons for our acts.
Their ends, our fears.
We are afraid
Because the dark is huge,
We are small.
Love is like a flame
And joy is warm.
We cannot come to harm
Accepting
All.

November 25, 1960
Thanksgiving Day

༚50༝

We Know All

We know not what we do, or why,
Or where we go. The clouds that blow
Across the sky may sooner know
Than we, who die.

November 26, 1960

∞51∞

In sorrow for not having telephoned before
Coming for a visit
And in joy for a card received

I fear that I shall never *see*
The knife
That you slip into me.
You'll ease it quiet in my back –
O life!
"Take it from me, dear Mack –
(The knife)"

Ugh! Oh!

Yet I love you so
(I'll warn you: now you know)
I'll take the knife
And strife –
But *bleed*
upon your toe.

December 9, 1960

∞52∞

Watch Out!

A first thought, written second, on contemplating a
victim nearly missed by knives and cannonballs.

There's another thought I owe to you
The thought that I can throw knives too.
I cause some pain, you surely see.
I'm sorry trouble comes with me.
Look out!
(Don't shout).
Just duck.
(Good luck!)

December 9, 1960

❦53❧

Saint Valentine's Day, 1961

Like the lightning I loved you,
dear.

Rumbling now,
On the clouds,
In the distance,
Or rain?

Like the lightning
I loved you!

Or still.

❧54❧

On Departing from Dubuque

I love you, Karen, from the humming plane
Above the silent fields, above the dusk.
A hidden lake gleams silver in the trees;
A mountainside is shadowed, still. In pain
my earth revolves. The sun falls redden
In her dignity and grace. The night surrounds
that image of your face I carry in my thoughts:
Your blue, blue eyes of clarity and peace, the joy
of your embrace. You lie so silent in my arms.
And by a mountain sheltered are from harms –
If I may to a mountain me compare
And you to darkness and to sun, to lake, to field:
All things that over me their beauty wield,
That teach me, far above, how much I love.

June 10, 1962

෨55෨

We Kneel Together, Dear

Together we enjoy the Christmas lights
Or is it, dear, the chillness of the nights?
Or is it dark? or silence?
Or the stars?
The fingered steeple
Peeks into the cold. My darling,
How I love you on my arm.
I love your footsteps sounding out
With mine. I love the breathing
Rhythm of your breasts,
And of your heart.
Oh!. . .you hear the chime?
You hear eternity? The dark?
We kneel together, dear.
The priest lifts up the Host.

Christmas, 1962

❦356❧

For Karen,
en route to England, as the Sun falls.

The plane throbs into night.
My sun falls on you now
(A redden band of light
Between the sea and dark),
And gives you, dear, my light.

Now as my night comes on I bid you send
To me the lightest spark
Of love: Until your sun returns
I am in night.

June 12, 1962

ೞ57ೞ

The Mountain & the Sun
for Karen

There is a mountain in my heart
Where clouds blow, gather, part.
Upon her peaks the snow gleams
Milky white; through pines the streams
Pull silver threads. The sky must bend
To glory her, bright stars descend
To glisten in her hair.
High in the hurrying, freshening air
Her shoulders block the night.
My mountainous Alp alone!
Stand silent! Strong! The light,
The day, creeps over you with love.

August 9, 1962

WASHINGTON

(1978–2010)

After several years as a tenured professor at the State University of New York at Old Westbury, at the Rockefeller Foundation, as a freelance writer, and the Ledden-Watson Chair at Syracuse University, Karen and I accepted the offer of a fellowship at the American Enterprise Institute. There followed thirty-two happy and creative years.

❦58❧

Are Seven Sounds Enough?
Exercises in –ough

A thorough cad from our borough
Long enough on a furlough
Broke the trough
With a bough
Through the rough
Wrecked his plough
And, needing bread, kneaded some dough

1983

ಡ59ಐ

Against the Sin of Gloattony

The least of deadly sins, old Dante said, is lust
   (A vice of Democratic presidential candidates, not
   winners.)

The second sin is avarice – more serious
   It is the vice that led the Lord himself to spurn
   Republicans and sinners.

The third deadly sin is gluttony
   Not a single time committed
   At any church-related dinners.

The worst of all deadly sins, old Dante said, is pride
   The sin of those who only go on ego trips
   And take all credit for the ride.

The fifth of deadly sins is envy
   Which possesses all a-ginners who hate the rich
   Or need
   To accuse of greed
   All who have what they would like to snitch.

The sixth deadly sin is sloth
   (I don't really care enough to find a rhyme for sloth.)

The Right's most deadly sin is gloattony
   Against which the IRD must specifically set its mind;
   For gloattony is our worse blight
   A pest attacking people of our kind
   When everything is going right.

So this my message is to IRD
On this most happy night:
"Resist the sin of gloattony
When all the world is going right!"

And going right it is, since 1981
When IRD was born.
In 1980 all the world was torn
When Soviet tanks attacked Afghanistan.
Angola, Ethiope', and Yemen felt the lash
And poor, poor Salvador was chosen for the clash
That had betrayed Managua's revolution –
Which the Sandinistas stole,
And all the Sandalistas
Swallowed whole.

But IRD was born, stood firm.
This tiny office, this little mouse,
Stampeded Riverside.
Brought down the house
That Marx built.

We did our job
And fought for right
And so I warn again tonight:
"Resist the sin of gloattony
When all the world is going right."

Forgive the NCC.
For shredding of the Iron Curtain, sing!
Enjoy the victory!
Let freedom's *glasnost* ring.

Enjoy the triumph of the West!
Democracies now come to power.

Religion met the test –
This is democracy's best hour.

We fought for this!
But too much bliss
Is gloattony.

And so, my friends, I warn again
On this most happy night
"Resist the sin of gloattony –
When all the world is going right."

Democracies on earth are few.
Religious freedom is as scarce as oil.
There's much to do
And much for which we still must toil.

So ah! my friends, and oh! our foes!
We all will sing this happy night:
"Resist the sin of gloattony
When all the world is going right."

October 8, 1991

Note: The IRD is the Institute for Religion and Democracy. The
NCC is the National Council of Churches.

☙60❧

The Ballad of RFE
For the old Board of International Broadcasting

Dim drums throbbing
On the hills half heard
Silence shatter
And the clatter
Of a thousand kettle drums

Awakens Christendom.
For the hammer and the sickle
In the darkness of the night
Have been marching, marching, marching
And there's going to be a fight.

All Europe is atremble
And the world stands back
In fear.
But all Europe needn't worry
And the world around should hear
That a rescuer is coming –
The USA is here.

In a faroff dell
In Washington
There is girding up a warrior
By the name of Eugene Pell.

Putting on his helmet
Taking up his spear;
Tying up his buckler

And hearing in his ear
The clearing throats of freedom
As the throats of freedom cheer.

A cheer that rents the night
Unsealing Europe's fate
And announces to the world
As the battle flag's unfurled
That Munich 1985
Isn't Munich '38
And there's going to be a fight.

The war that might be fought
Is terrible to face
For under nuclear assault
All Europe could lie waste.
Or if twelve million men
From every nation fair
Were hurled into the battle
In their tanks and battle gear –
Not a nation would be standing
Not a home would battle spare
And all Europe would lie ruined
And all Europe would be bare.

So the strategy is simple
But the doing of it's hell –
It's fight the war with Radio
And in the end game Eugene Pell.
It's fight the war with Radio
Under America's Gene Pell.

For Radio is not a bomb
And it doesn't move with tanks.

It isn't General Patton
Or the old Field Marshall Rommel
Appearing on the flanks.
It isn't General Zhukov
Rockets, planes, or subs.
It's simply words and concepts,
Ideas and symbols– sound–
The sound of human voices
And the souls these voices found.

Eastern Europe's huddled masses
Yearning to breathe free
Were forbidden to think freely
Or to say what freedom thought.
Forgotten nations, sadly,
Where hope was daily tested
And being captive seemed their lot.

The Polish sky seemed leaden
The Slovak sky was grey
So also those of Budapest
And Prague and Minsk. (They say
The color best for Communism
Wasn't red but grey.)
Yet though the light could not the mist dispel
Waves of sound could find a way
To heat the inner souls of men
And hold the mist at bay.

Lech Walesa, that tectic hero he,
Of electricity
Electrified the silent peoples
Made them glow
And showed the world new ways to go.

But how could people Lech Walesa hear
Four decades long had lived in fear?
Alone at night, their family near,
Through static, jamming, darkness blear,
They heard the voice of freedom clear.
The solidarity that's in the soul
First enters through the human ear.
"Faith comes by hearing," said St. Paul,
Radio Free Europe held that dear.
"It was our sun!" Walesa said,
"It brought the day of freedom here."

When Europe still in darkness lay
And Lech Walesa's shipyard still lay bleak
Arrived in Munich one grey week
A radio man *extraordinaire*
Whose mission was to take the air
And bring the Iron Curtain down.
And while you're at it, lies dispel –
While you're at it, lies dispel.
That's what his bosses said
To Eugene Pell.
Lies dispel
And bring the Iron Curtain down.

And so we gather here, dear sir,
To give you thanks.
You did as you were told.
You did it under budget, but gold
Wasn't mostly what you saved –
Liberty it was you braved
The odds to take to every heart
In Europe, and hearts there beat today
With gratitude

That you were where you were,
Did what you did, kind sir.

We honor you tonight
For carrying forward one good fight!
We honor well th'imagination
You brought to serve your nation
And the world.
800 numbers, who'd a thought it?
That Communists would call collect
To get fresh information on the air,
As did the stringers you had hired everywhere.
The Cold War was over when you fought it
With ideas.

The Iron Curtain falls in tatters
When the iron will of leaders shatters
And nothing moves the will like truth
Which you put on the air,
Double sourcing Chernobyl,
And getting your facts right when others fell.
You served your country well,
Eugene Pell.
You served your country well.

Tonight we say our thanks.
You conquered Europe, not with tanks
But with the radio.
You were the sun.
Lech Walesa was the one to say so.
You did as you were told
Your word was good as gold –
By working hard in Munich town,
Not alone, you brought the Iron Curtain down

You did the lies dispel.
You served your country well,
Eugene Pell.
You served your country well.

December 18, 1996

∞61∞

On Being Libertarian

Admirers may think of them
As Murray One and Murray Two
Here Charles is better known
But Arthur was a Murray, too.

How Arthur Murray danced! He'd glide
Across the floor
And thrill the hearts of every girl
That entered in the door.

Charles is an artist, too, though writing
Is his forte –
While Arthur danced, young Charles is known
To be the thinking sort.

Out on the left he started out;
But in Cambodia – or maybe was it Thailand –
His thinking changed. The statist world
For him lost all its clout.
It did not work.
He rediscovered Edmund Burke.

Just when you thought he
Might be *Losing Ground*
Charles rode *The Curve of Bell* around
And while P.C. sank ever deeper root
In sappiness
He wrote instead
Pursuit of Happiness.

Charles never liked
The statist status quo – 'twas so
The little libertarian in him did grow.

What did it mean for Charles
To be a Libertarian?
He didn't know.
He couldn't find a definition
So he could quote it.
He couldn't find a book
And so he wrote it.

Now many people are confused these days
A clear idea – they never get one.
For all they know, a libertarian
May have as kin utilitarian,
Rotarian, or even Rastafarian –
They never met a one.

As Richard Nixon said one day,
"We are all Keynesians now."
But he was wrong.
We all are freedom's children now
And Charles has written freedom's song.

Charles is not a libertarian-upper-case
Oh no!
The kind of libertarian he is
Is low. The kind that says "Gee whiz!
I love my family, town, and work.
I can't abandon Edmund Burke.
While free I want to be
It's only fun with my community!"

So you can see that he
Is better called a Whig:
A libertarian-Whig
Or Whiggish libertarian
More sworn to law
Than just utilitarian.

His image of the law
Is like the Lady in the Harbor – arm upraised
A lantern held aloft like reason's light
To cut through fog and mist unfazed.
The lantern is not all the Lady took.
In her other hand, she held a book
Of law: Liberty under reason
And in every season also under law.
A Whiggish view of liberty,
Under God and under Law:
Nations guided by the prod
Of nature's law and nature's God.

I hope it has as many readers
As the Park Jurassic
And do not hesitate to give its mark –
A classic.

January 14, 1997

ເ362ໄ

Friends Around Your Table
For Jude and Pat

Congratulations, Jude and Pat!
To both of you, all tip a hat
For forty years now, you've been wed!
Around your table, it's been said,
– We guess ten thousand friends you've fed:
Rocco, Tischner, Paolo, Russ
Dr. Langan, Ralph, and Gus,
Sokolowski, Rauscher – us!
Your boys would help – and Jude might cook –
But did it Pat's way: by the book.
For Queen Patricia ruled o'er all
(She seemed to hold the Dean in thrall)
If Jude, with apron on, would joke,
Well, Pat would raise her eyes, and smoke.

Oh! Jude our Dean, and Pat our Queen
Your friends for both of you are keen!
Yours was our favorite 'Beltway' table
You warmed as no one else was able.
Your friendship is among our joys!
We honor you for your great boys:
How many blessings you have seen,
Oh! Jude our Dean! And Pat our Queen!

You may think forty years a lot
But take with you this closing thought:

Your sons, your friends, their cups upraise –
To tell you "Thanks!" And sing your praise!

Best Wishes,
Michael and Karen Novak

January 4, 1998

ᏃᎾ63ᏑᎾ

Upon Your Ordination

God often does His work in quiet ways and chooses quiet guys
And Derek Cross if nothing else is quiet as the skies
As clouds scud past the sun. But he is also wise
As those will see who break through his disguise.

I think I've known him longer now than anyone who's here
Except for Mom and Dad – who now deserve a cheer!
And many thanks from all of us for giving back their son
To the Maker of the stars and moon and sun!

And to the Bishop who ordained him, and the Pastor of St. Joe's
And Father Robert, friends, and cooks, and every one of those
Who gathers here together to share this day of laud –
When Derek Cross of Maryland became a priest of God.

God often does His work in quiet ways and chooses quiet guys
And Derek Cross if nothing else is quiet as he's wise.
Today God has ordained him for a future of great things
And all the world around us of his grace and talent sings.

So let us raise our glasses in a toast to Derek Cross
Whom God has chosen plainly for a privileged grace today.
And thank the Lord Who chose him, Who cut away the dross,
And put the gold in Derek, before His people to display!

Congratulations!

June 1998

⊗64⊗

Hers Too, You!

Top Hat Chimney had descended from our roof
When Billie Jean the hippie divorcee
Who lived across the street
Asked him to come inspect her chimney
The Top Hat truck remained outside her home three days
And when he exited a smile played on his face
Hers too, you!

March 1998

♋365♌

The Ballad of Richard John
(G. K. Chesterton, Again!)

An Explanatory Note:

In the year of Our Lord 1571, an enormous Muslim fleet under the command of Admiral Ali and the authority of Sultan Selim II swept the Eastern Mediterranean and, by autumn, was harboring in the Greek Isles trying to lure into battle what remained of the Christian fleet, preparatory to an unimpeded sweep up the Italian coast to conquer Italy. Lassitude gripped the Kings of Spain, France and Italy and the Queen of England; few Christian warriors stirred. If Selim II took Italy and Spain, Christian culture in Europe would go dark. Only one Christian Prince recognized the danger, Don Juan of Austria, and behind him rallied a few great warriors, and the few remaining vessels of the Knights of Malta, undaunted by being vastly outnumbered and outgunned. As the Christian fleet sailed toward the Gulf of Lepanto off the southern coast of Greece, in circumstances Selim II considered very favorable to his vast forces, Pope Pius V was urging all Christians to say the rosary incessantly on behalf of victory in this hour of sore need.

On the morning of October 7, 1571, the Christian fleet rowed boldly into the center of the Saracen fleet, in whose bowels thousands of Christian prisoners toiled under the lash at the Saracen oars. The wind speeded the Muslim fleet, and rendered the Christian sails useless until at the last moment it reversed direction. The Saracen sails drooped, their ships stopped dead in the water, and the Christian fleet bore into them with great force – and the confidence of feeling the wind of God in their sails.

The Christian slaves at the Muslim oars were itching for rebellion. When the wind blew strong behind them and their oars were slack, those in the holds of the Muslim right flank used the time to loosen their manacles, and as the Christian ships grappled alongside, they raced up above deck swinging their chains as men desperate for liberty. Attacked from fore and aft, the crews on the decks of the Muslim right flank were soon demoralized. Every single Muslim ship on that flank was sunk or captured.

Gilbert Keith Chesterton wrote his celebrated ballad "Lepanto" to honor that day's events. I hope that in heaven he forgives me for the parody. He would certainly concur in honoring Richard John Neuhaus.

Dim drums throbbing on the hills half heard,
At one-five-six Fifth Avenue a balding prince has stirred
And, risen from his swivel chair and editorial stall,
The last knight of America takes weapons from the wall.
The last and lingering troubadour (for whom the Pope has
    rung),
That once grew up in Canada when all the world was young.
In that enormous silence, tiny and unafraid,
Comes down along the Avenue a new type of Crusade.
Strong gongs groaning as his fax booms far,
Richard John of *First Things* is marching down to war,
Stiff flags straining in the night-blasts cold,
In the gloom black-purple, in the glint old-gold,
Torchlight crimson on the copper kettle-drums,
Then the tuckets, then the trumpets, then computer, and he
    comes.
Richard John laughing with his brave hair curled,
Rising in his stirrups 'gainst the thrones of all the world,
And holding up his head as if the flag of all the free.
Love-light of Neo-cons!
Pen pal of Schindler's dons!
Death-light to Naked Squares!
Paragon of Brian Hehir's!
Richard John of First Things
Is riding to the sea.

St. Patrick's on Fifth Avenue but twenty blocks to north
(Richard John of First Things is girt and going forth.)
Times Square's aglitter and the sharp tides shift
As the journalists catch breezes and their red sails lift.
He fills his pen with deadly ink and he claps his laptop
    closed;
The noise has rung through Gotham; indifferent Gotham
    dozed.

That City's full of tangled things and texts and aching eyes,
And dead are all its innocents, all slain before they rise,
As Christian killeth Christian in a well-lit clinic room,
And Christian dreadeth Christ that hath a newer face of
    doom,
And they abandon Mary, that God kissed in Galilee –
The God who stooped to pick up dust and blow into it breath,
For they have stomped their feet on life, and made their cul-
    ture Death.
So Richard John of First Things is riding to the sea.
Richard John is calling through the blast and the eclipse
Crying through the trumpet, the trumpet of his lips,
And his trumpet cryeth "Ha!
Domino sit gloria!"
Richard John of First Things
Is pointing to the ships.

ii

The Cardinal's in his office with his cross about his neck
(Richard John of First Things is armed upon the deck.)
His prayers are with his brother priest out on the salty sea,
The Pope has urged the world around to pray the rosary,
To say the beads both night and day for no man can tell how
The Christian fleet can conquer Death, whose fleet from prow
    to prow
Now fills the sea around in numbers two to one,
And taller, faster, better armed, two guns per Christian gun.
And murder's on the Sultan's lips and gleam lights up his
    eyes.
In emeralds and silks he thinks, "No Christian is our worth.
Put down our feet upon their throats that peace be on this
    earth."
And so begins October day, and so begins his work,
As Richard John of First Things now fires on the Turk.

Richard John is hunting, and his hounds they now have bayed
—

Booms away to Italy the rumor of his raid.
Gun upon gun, ha! ha!
Gun upon gun, hurrah!
Richard John of First Things
Has loosed the cannonade.

The Pope was in his chapel as day and battle broke
(Richard John of First Things is hidden in the smoke.)
That hidden room in man's house where God sits all the year,
The secret window where the world looks small – and very
      dear.
He sees as in a mirror in the monstrous morning's breath
The crescent of the hostile ships whose culture's name is
      Death;
They fling great shadows foe-wards, making Cross and *First
      Things* dark,
They veil the pluméd lions on the galleys of St. Mark.
Aboard their hostile ships are learned, educated chiefs,
Below the decks are prisoners with multitudinous griefs,
Infant captives sick and sunless, all a laboring race repines
Like a race in sunken cities, like a nation in the mines.
They are lost like slaves that sweat, and in the skies of
      morning hung
The stairways of the tallest gods when tyranny was young.
They are countless, voiceless, hopeless as those fallen fleeing
      on
The distant granite pavements of their exile Babylon.
And many a one will struggle in his quiet room in hell
As a surgeon's face looks grimly through the lattice of his
      cell,
As he finds his God is silent, as he seeks no more a sign –
(But Richard John of First Things has burst the battle line!)

iii

They rush in red and purple from the red clouds of the morn
From temples where the gods of Death shut up their eyes in
    scorn
And the wind puffs up the Sultan's sails and his aggressive
    pride –
Oak oars straining on the groaning Christian side.
Straining, too, the warriors' eyes
Study foe ahead
Closing seas, blood-red skies,
At last mad cries of battle rise –
...The wind stops dead.
Turns, now fills the Christian weal,
Clatter down the Sultan's sails,
Back the Sultan's sailors reel.
(Boom! go the Christian guns, let fly the Muslim bow)
Below the decks roar sergeants' shouts,
"Row, ye Christian slaves from hell! Row!
These lashes tell ye, row!"
Slaves have shaken shackles free
Swinging chains, girt at the loin,
They burst out of the stinking hold
As with a clatter and a fury the wild ships of Venice join.
Blood flows purple as the flesh grows cold.
Undone, Mohammed's right,
As ship by ship yields up the will to fight.
Ten thousand turbans float upon the sea
As on th'embattled Sultan's flagship
Don Juan slays Ali.

So Richard John goes pounding on the slaughter-painted
    poop,
Purpling all the ocean like a bloody pirate's sloop,
Scarlet running over on the silvers and the golds,

Breaking of the hatches up and bursting of the holds,
Thronging of the thousands up that labor under sea
White for bliss and blind for sun and stunned for liberty.
Life a Te Deum sings!
Praise all the King of Kings!
Richard John of First Things
Has set his people free!

                              iv
Cervantes on his galley sets the sword back in the sheath
(Richard John of First Things rides homeward with a wreath.)
He sees across a weary past a straggling road in Spain,
Up which a lean and foolish knight Quixote rides in vain.
Cervantes smiles, as writers smile, and settles back the
        blade...

And Richard John of First Things rides home from his
        Crusade.
He tells his crews this message, which I mark down in my
        book:
"We'll turn this thing around, my friends –
 Just turn your head and look.
Our foes are fierce, and o! they boast!
But you can tell them now, my friends,
In Richard's eyes, they're toast!"

And so it is throughout the world
Where Richard's flag's unfurled,
The word goes out from his crusade,
"My friends, BE NOT AFRAID!"

Pius V pronounced these words as Prince Don Juan of Austria
        entered before him at the Vatican after the victory: *"Fuit
        Homo missus a Deo cui nomen erat Joannes."* I will trans-

late this freely, to reflect our collective judgment about our friend and honoree: In our time of need, "There was a man sent by God whose name was Richard John."

Union League Club,
October 12, 1999
Youth for the Third Millennium Award to
Richard John Neuhaus

ଓଽ66ଃ

Dear Marjorie

With how much affection we think of you
With what pleasure we recall meeting you and Jim
and young family at Aspen and elsewhere down the years –
Dinner at your home, dinner at ours.
It must have been thirty years ago that we first met.
We remember laughing a lot together, even then –
Sharing so many views in common – about the state of the
nation, and culture, and matters of faith,
not to mention issues of religion in Russia and the
long accumulated crumbling of the Berlin Wall and the Soviet
   will.

We've lived so much of life as friends,
Seen the world change around us more than once,
Watched our children grow into such amazing adults,
Taken pleasure in the workings of Providence on behalf of
   our country
(now as always before in our people's past).
Thank you for being you – your eyes are always so curious
your laughter so quick.
You were always so much fun to tease – you believed
Everything we said (when we were just kidding) until you
   caught us
and laughed along with everyone else. Your goodness guided
   you.
You have been a pure good in our lives.

Michael and Karen Novak   2000

☙67❧

Cromartie at Fifty –
A Verse for a Basketball Widow

I think it's pretty nifty
That Cromartie is fifty.
But better yet –
Is the swish of the net –
When the little guy gets shifty.

Now I've heard of guys who love to play
There are lots of them in this nation
But most are willing to call it a day
When their knee has an operation.

Not this guy
With a heart like the sky
And with moves that will catch you napping
He jumps toward the net –
Off his fingers the ball –
High arch, swift fall, net's snapping.

Some men quake at the mention of knife
But Cromartie's fear is the loss of his life
If he can't throw up more jump shots.
He's taken the knife three times to his knee
And he's still throwing up jump shots.
Out from the circle are his favorite spots
But his deadliest drops from the key.

Oh, I've been his friend for a dozen years
And I've never seen his spirits flag.
So I offer a toast to the man of the hour
In the form of a friendly gag:
"For your work in the future,
My dear, dear friend, you'll gather a pretty penny.
But the best thing you ever caught in your net
Is the wise and ebullient Jenny!"

August 2000

ೞ68ೲ

Our Friend George is Fifty

Our friend George
Is fifty years of age.
Our friend George
A good man is and sage.

Our friend George
Has lived for fifty years.
Let's wish him happy birthday now
And raise high fifty beers!

The story of the greatest pope
His calling was to write.
He saw him as a star of hope
In the darkness of the night.

He sat at Pope Wojtyla's feet
Whose words were steeled in fire.
Like ingots in a white-hot heat
The Lord Jesus did inspire.

A work of art did George acquit
A glory of our land.
An honor for his friends it is
To be in George's band!

Our friend George
Has lived for fifty years.
Let's wish him happy birthday now
And raise high fifty beers!

These days it is not possible
For the Pope to make George Cardinal.
It doesn't matter anyhow –
He's fifty years an Oriole!

Our friend George
Has lived for fifty years.
So – let's wish him happy birthday now
And raise high fifty beers!

May 6, 2001

His Jokes Rock the Heavens with Laughter
*A Verse For Monsignor Timothy Dolan, Bishop-elect,
on the 25th anniversary of his priestly ordination.
(Heavily borrowed from Rudyard Kipling "L'Envoi")*

When a Bishop's last picture is painted, and his
      tubes are twisted and dried,
When the oldest colors have faded, and the
      youngest critic has died,
He shall rest, and, faith, he shall need it – lie
      down for an eon or two,
Till the Master of All Good Workmen shall set him
      to work anew!

Bishop Tim if he's good shall be happy: he
      shall sit in a golden chair;
He shall splash at a ten-league canvas with
      rushes of comet's hair;
He shall find real saints to draw from –
      Magdalene, Peter, and Paul;
He shall work for an age at a sitting and never
      be tired at all!

And only the Master shall praise him, and only
      the Master shall blame;
Father Tim never worked for the money, Father Tim
      never worked for the fame;
He worked for the joy of the working, and reached
      for his separate star,
He drew all Things as he saw Them for the God of
      Things as They Are!

He shall live for ever and ever, but today
      he's our new rising star;
His fam'ly and friends wish him blessings, his enemies
      sulk from afar,
But his jokes rock the heavens with laughter, Father Tim
      is our new rising star.

                   June 2001

[Father Tim was made Bishop of Milwaukee in 2002, and Archbishop of New York in 2009.]

ೞ70ൣ

Michael Joyce!
A Ballad Composed for June 11, 2001.
A Celebration at the 21 Club, Manhattan
In Honor of the Best Amongst the Brothers
(Abject apologies to Rudyard Kipling – "Gunga Din")

You can talk th' blarney when yer
In a job with tenure
An' yer writin' book reviews for pleasure.
But then y'r wife had chillen
An' you faced th' sinkin' feelin'
You mus' surrender to the rat-race pressure –
But you wanted to spend time
In an optimistic clime,
A-servin' wi' th' Irving Kristol boys!
(Of all that bloomin' crew
The finest man ya knew
Was your regimental leader, Michael Joyce!)

He was "Joyce! Joyce! Joyce!
You limpin' lump of Erin, Michael Joyce!
Idea for ya– ya like it?
The money, can ya maike it?
You leprechaun o' Eire, Michael Joyce!"

Th'appearance that he wore
Was nothin' much before
An' rather more it 'umble wuz than proud
But ya knew he had a mind
That sharp wuz, o' th' kind
That kissed the sod and hated fuzzy cloud.

When McGovern's legions lay
Their red-hot fire down one day.
When 'better red than dead' made 'ilton's bloomin' eyebrows
       crawl
We shouted "Michael Joyce!"
Though our throats could not be moist,
An' 'e 'elped us, tho' he couldn't fund us all.

It was "Joyce! Joyce! Joyce!
Yo Erin, don't ya ever hear the noise?
Hurry! Need your help! Be quick
Or they'll give us quite a lick
If you don't come through with money, Michael Joyce!"

'E would duck an' work inside
Till we finally turned the tide;
An' 'e didn't seem to know the use o' fear.
If we charged or broke or cut,
You could bet your bloomin' butt,
'E'd be bringin' up the money from the rear.
With his weapon off 'is back,
'E would join in our attack,
An' fire till the bugles blew "Retire."
Yet for all 'is Irish 'ide,
He had soul, pure mensch, inside
When 'e went to tend the wounded under fire!

It was "Joyce! Joyce! Joyce!"
With the lefties hurlin' charges at the boys.
When our cartridges ran out,
You could hear our front ranks shout,
"Hey! Ammunition mules, you! Michael Joyce!"

I shan't forget the night
When I dropped be'ind the fight

110

With a bullet where my belt plate made a noise.
I was chokin' mad with thirst,
An' the man that spied me first
Was our good old fightin' Irish Michael Joyce.
'E lifted up me 'ead,
An' he plugged me where I bled,
An' he guv me lots o' reasons to rejoice:
I was stinkin', down, an' 'ot,
An' so, of salaries I've got
I'm gratefullest to one from Michael Joyce.

It was "Joyce! Joyce! Joyce!
'Ere's a beggar who 'as fallen in th' noise,
'E's chawin' up the ground,
An' 'e's kickin' all around:
Fur Gawd's sake find the money, Michael Joyce!"

'E kept us in the fight
Through the battles of the night.
But the bullets flew at 'im, too, i' th' noise.
'E took us to the top
An' just before we drop,
"I 'ope my efforts helped," sez Michael Joyce.

So if we meet 'im later on
At a place where we've all gone,
 Where it's always lefties win (and none rejoice);
'E'll be squattin' on the coals
Givin' grants to poor damned souls–
We'll all get grants in hell from Michael Joyce!

Yes, Joyce! Joyce! Joyce!
You Leprechaun o' Erin Michael Joyce!
Though we've roasted you and braised you,

By the livin' Gawd that raised you,
You're the best man 'mongst our brothers, Michael Joyce!

June 11, 2001

࿇71࿇

Free At Last, Scott Walter, Free At Last
In Honor of Scott Walter's Eighteen Years of Yeoman Service

Scott began to work for me in 1983.
A Hoya Sophomore then, as bright as he could be.
"You'll think that Scott's read everything," reported Father
  Schall.
"If Sister Eve an apple bit, Scott ate the whole darn tree."

In three years Scott his BA won, and stayed to work some
  more.
He looked up facts, selected quotes, while books o'erflowed
  his floor.
He helped me launch a magazine – the name we chose was
  Crisis –
Attacking democratic soc'alism wi' Hayek and Von Mises.

He called up Walker Percy once, and asked him to contribute –
That final interview he gave to Scott was Percy's highest
  tribute.
Scott next conceived an interview with novelist Tom Clancy.
Scott really had no fears, you see, and called who pleased his
  fancy.

After this apprenticeship, Scott r'turned to AEI,
And beamed the starship Enterprise, up far beyond the sky.
A perfect gentleman is Scott: Brooks Brothers, bourbon neat,
A Georgia-sweet mint julep, Tennessee beneath his feet.

As God my humble self did use to launch Scott's working life,
He used me once again to hire the beauty who is Scott's wife.

113

And my return, my friends, is a priceless, precious surety –
Erica and Scott gave birth to save my Soch' Security.

I am happy, friends, for Erica, Scott, and Henry at the mast.
Now after almost twenty years Scott will be free at last –
But not too free, as you can see. He may walk out the doors –
But we will see him often, still. He's only down five floors!

October 26, 2001

Saint Henry's Day
In Honor of Henry Hyde

Against the odds–

> It was important during the winter of 1998 for someone in the
> Congress to uphold the Law– and the Honor of our people. As in so
> many things, William Shakespeare has best expressed the thoughts of
> our Prince Hal, our own King Henry, on the eve of Henry's Day, Year
> of our Lord, 2001. With very few amendments, I quote as follows:

If we are mark'd to lose, we are enow
To do our country loss, and if to win,
The fewer men, the greater share of honor.
By Jove, I am not covetous for gold,
Nor care I who doth feed upon my cost.
It yearns me not if men my garments mock;
Such outward things dwell not in my desires.
But if it be a sin to covet honor,
I am the most offending soul alive.
God's peace! I would not lose so great an honor
As such another man would share from me
I' this best fight for law. Wish not another!
Nay, broadcast this throughout the land
That he which hath no stomach to this fight,
Let him depart. His passport shall be made
And campaign funding put into his purse.
We would not fight in that man's company
That has no heart to fight for law.

This day is called among us Henry's Day.
He that outlives this day and comes safe home

Will stand a-tiptoe when this day is named
And rouse him at the name of Henry Hyde.
He that shall see this day and live old age
Will yearly on the vigil nudge his friends
And say 'Tomorrow, coz, is Henry's Day.'
Then will he pull his book and show his clips,
[And say 'These stripes I took on Henry's Day.']
Old men forget; but scorn be not forgot,
And he'll remember with advantages
What barbs he took that day. Then shall our names,
Familiar in his mouth as household words –
Henry the King, Rogan and Hutchinson,
Canaday, Cannon, McCollum, Lindsay Graham and –
Gekas, Chabot, Bryant, Buyer, Barr – all these.
Be in their flowing cups freshly remember'd.
This story shall the good man teach his son
About the rule of law, and truth, and how
The great are bound by law as are the low,
And honor is an em'rald island in a speckled sea.

And Henry's Day shall ne'er go by
From this day to the ending of the world,
But we in it shall be remembered –
We few, we happy few, we band of brothers.
For he that day that stood his ground with me
Became my brother. Be he e'er so low,
That day did gentle his condition.

And senators in this land now abed
Shall rue until their *Dies Irae* day –
And hold their manhoods cheap – that they
Fought not with Henry on St. Henry's Day.

Institute for Psychological Sciences
November 7, 2001

☙73☜

Sweet Grattan Brown

Twas 9/11/2-0-0-1 when Grattan came to town
And he's said since then that after that, he went nowhere but
    down.
For more than two years – almost three – he couldn't please
    his boss.
No matter how much work he did, how well, how quick, his
    cross
Old boss would search for something he'd done wrong.
Now you might think, good friends, that this would get him
    down . . .
But not so Grattan Brown, my friends – it made him burst in
    song:

> Swee-eet Grattan Brown!
> It can't be me, it ain't my fault,
> I do good work, of earth the salt,
> Oh, I'm sweet Grattan Brown.

Today's the day, that's overdue, when Grattan Brown breaks
    free!
Emanci-pa-tion pro-clamation, folks, is what this day will be –
He did his work, he did great work, a LOT of work did he!
About a dozen major lectures, letters by the score,
Murray dinners, monthly lunches for the press, and more –
(Freedom of the press, he learned, means lunch for them is
    free) –
Institute in Krakow, the Slovak Seminar – events he had to
    plan.

At times the lives of galley slaves seemed attractive to this
man.
He learned to proofread galleys, he learned research, we
wrote a book –
(A lot of re-writes, corrections, drafts, that took!)

Swee-eet Grattan Brown!
He is the best, up to the sky,
Today he's free, I'll miss this guy,
Oh, he's sweet Grattan Brown!

June 18, 2004

࿇74࿇

My Cousin Pat

My Cousin Pat is suffering
Please pray for her.
She lost her husband only months ago,
And it has hit her hard.
Spent she feels, and desolate –
As if with nothing more to give.
Death has left her feeling empty
She loved him so.
She broke out into tears
Without a reason
(It is unlike her).

Every time she passes streets
Where once they walked
A counter, even, in the hardware store
Where once they stopped
She misses standing close to him
Aroma of his pipe
His love of music –
All those shelves of records
Go unplayed.

At eighteen, Pat was in a contest crowned
Miss Dearborn
Celebrated for her beauty and her soul.
Soft she is, considerate, tender, sweet,
Yet also steely tough.
Her vocation was to be a nurse –

Unshaken at the worst was she
Unshakeable no matter what
The crisis be, or urgency,
Or blood.

Determination is her middle name.
"Determination Plus" I call her.
When you see her right lip tighten
Up into a pretty little dimple –
Stand not in her way.
It means that she means business,
And she will never, ever sway,
Never deviate.

Soft she is, and iron tough,
Quiet, willful, sweeter far than sweet.
Yet our dear Pat, so quick to smile,
Is overcome with grief
And something more than grief.
Exhaustion of the soul.
She may be strong, and fit,
Energetic, smiling often.
But those who know her know it:
Antarctica is what she feels like.
Or Sahara?
Places desolate, and empty, chill.
They make her shiver so
One wants to hug her
To warm her up
But it is better not to do that yet,
Let the grieving run its course.

Yet don't forget to pray for her,
Surround her, cover her with prayer,

Bury her in petals, St. Therese,
Who being on the darkest nights deserted
Kept loving Christ –
And through him all the world.

Darkness and emptiness
Are not to be afraid of,
They are our friends.
They lead us into blindness,
Into emptiness,
Where alone God can be found.
Listen! Listen!
Be still. Be calm.
And turn your will toward Him.
Say *Yes* to what He sends.
The storm will pass.

And Pat will be the sweeter for it.
Tougher, too,
And mightily determined
As she always is.
Her empty heart will overflow
With God's own love
(No need for hers).
Where she feels empty
God will fill.

I send her, too, a cousin's love.
Amen

2005

C875JO

In Memory of Oriana Fallaci
(1929–2006)

Oriana! Oriana!
Your very name
Lifts us to the rising of the sun

Incandescent presence
In a world gone dark

How much you loved
your native, your beloved, Florence!

Loved its Duomo
Its Baptistery
Its David
Its tormented Michelangelos
In the Salas of the Medici

Loved Santa Croce
The Uffizi, Pitti
Convent of the Fra Angelicos
The Bridge across the Arno

Loved cafes
and cappuccinos
and – oh, sadly, yes – cigarettes'
candescent glows
and wisps of silver in the night.

Brave soul,
You strengthened us,
You steadied us,
Embattled for our very lives

We loved you, Oriana,
In loving you, we loved
The best
Beyond ourselves.

October 2006

೮376ೞ

Chuck Colson at Seventy-Five

Chuck Colson is a gold, gold train
  Whooshing toward the Light –
  Colson Colson Colson **Colson**
  Colson Colson Colson **Colson**
  Shrieking through the night.

    A Harvard man,
  A ramrod straight marine,
    He turned to law
    But seeing much,
  He never really saw.

    Oh, he was smart
  And he was tough
    And – maybe –
  Just a little rough.

    In all the glory
  Of the White House days –
    He could not see
  The bridge was out –
    Ahead a blaze.

  His train once wrecked,
  He took it like a man.
And found in prison Jesus Christ
    His Lord
  Beyond all riches prized.

To prisoners accursed,
Armed with the Word,
Chuck preached his Lord
(As then, so now, the Same).
Upon the dying sparks he blew
Until the graying embers burst
Like blood upon a star –
And spirits burst aflame.

Like Wilberforce, like Wilberforce
Chuck set the prisoners free
And yet, and yet, it was not he,
Not Chuck who was the Source
But Holy Spirit, Father, Son,
Communion of Three.

(Non nobis, Domine, non nobis,
Sed Nomini Tuo da gloriam!)
Not to Chuck, O Lord, and not to us,
Unto Thy Name be glory!

Chuck is a friend
A kindly man
In whom God's love does shine
We know him through the broken bread
And the drinking of the wine.

Chuck is a force for unity
Among all Christian folk
A spokesman for philosophy
To frame the words God spoke.

It's good, O Lord, to be alive –
And praise Thee, thank Thee, love Thee –
As Chuck roars through the Station,
Seventy, and five.

October 19, 2006

ᏆᏆ

Seamus at Fifty

Seamus Ernesto Hasson is a hunter o' Bear.
(Seamus Ernesto Hasson takes life as a dare.)
When his beard is full, and shaped as he likes
He looks like that novelist eyeing his bull
Who in his love poem to Spain, "For Whom the Bell Tolls" –
Is whipping his cape for the Roar running past
When horn scratches his rib-cage – just at the last.
Whose novel of war "The Sun Also Rises"
Gave Seamus our leader his love for surprises.

I can remember "Friend" Parkinson shaking his hand –
So that year for his birthday Seamus longed for a stand
In front of a Bear too heavy to haul,
Whose eyes red with malice, anger, and gall
Glared at our hero and charged straight ahead,
While Seamus whose fingers were calm and up high
Squeezed on his trigger –
And down went the Big Bear,
Down big, and then bigger,
A giant of fur, meat – and bleeding right eye.

That, my dear friends, is Seamus on birthdays.
No cake does he want, no candles to blow,
But a trigger to pull, a true shot to let whiz
When the teeth of the monster are beginning to drool
And the glare of Bear eyes meets the steel blue of his.
(Seamus Ernesto Hasson takes life as a dare.)
The Becket Fund is a new die he has thrown in the air –

127

So I have advice for the ACLU:
Stay away from his trigger
Or he'll shoot you through.

May 2007

ᭀᔆ78ᔆᩏ

Christopher, Farewell! –
And Come Join the Fun!

I.

Christopher,
Christopher,
Christopher True!

You –

      Made AEI a most happy place
      Brought in some red-hot new Fellows
      Picked out an all-stellar staff
      Raised boat loads of money

You've –

      A quick eye for what's funny
      And a true roaring laugh

You're –

      Unflappable, even-tempered, never seem to be blue
      Christopher, Christopher, Christopher True.

II.

While the rest of us played, you looked over our wall –
Pulled back by meetings, budgets, one more phone call.
Christopher, Christopher, Christopher Good,
When you coulda or woulda, always did what you should.
For twenty-one years you labored for us.

129

Never heard you angry, never heard you cuss.
The best good of all that you did with such grace –
You made AEI a most happy place.
A miracle THAT is, with professors and such.
Held a minimum of meetings, used red tape not much.
A lawyer, you lawyered a very good case.
You loved J.S. Bach, with a very deft touch,
The Mass of St. Matthew, organ solos, cantatas apace –
You did everything Bach-wards – which accounts for your
    balance,
Your measure, your grace.

III.

Christopher, Christopher, Christopher Brave,
When our life was fading, when our hopes were low,
You came with a lifeline, our future helped save.
With cheeriness and laughter you labored below
Knew everyone's first name, knew everyone's face
YOU MADE AEI A MOST HAPPY PLACE!

Christopher, Christopher, after twenty-one years
Bach's angels are singing:
"Drop weights from your shoulders,
Come into the sun!
Come read, come write –
Come join the fun!"

IV.

Someplace, somewhere, on a green rolling hill
Bright sunlight will shine on a tombstone so still
"HERE lies Christopher, Christopher, – Brave, Good and
    True.

He labored with Bach's grace
He made AEI
A MOST HAPPY PLACE."

October 12, 2007

ᎧᏒ79ᏽᎣ

The Wedding of John and Jana
A Toast in Verse

Jana began, as children should, in love –
Her mother's and her father's.
She did not come from me alone
Nor only from her mother.
But from us both she was, she is,
In independent unison.

Careful, John. Know this:
Perfectionist she is like both of us.
Like both, she can be fierce –
And loving, too, can like her mother
Sweetness bring, your heart to pierce.

Sweet she is, but like hard marble
Is her *will*.
Her will she gives you, John,
So love her, love her
As she has been loved.
And she will love you
Now, forevermore.

She has a *mind* as sharp as diamonds
Are, that cut Carrara's stones –
Those white-glare blocks the chisel hones
To David, Moses, and the Pietà.

It took a special type of man to win our Jana's heart,
And be given thus her heart to hold.

Mature he had to be, and brave,
And it did not hurt him to have Purple Hearts,
Two in fact, or that he had been fired at
On every continent except Antarctica
In the service of his country.

Dear family, friends – I speak the truth:
These two, like magnets drawn
Whose independence did not want to tire
(As iron ingots do not fuse except in white-hot fire)
Which, once achieved, they are at peace.

Resisted they not once, not twice, but many times
Until, assured the bond unbroken
E're would be,
Surrendered they in unity.

Jana began, as children should, in love –
Her mother's and her father's.
She did not come from me alone
Nor only from her mother.
But from us both she came, she is,
In independent unison.

Perfectionist she is, like both.
Like both, she can be fierce –
And loving, too, can like her mother
Sweetness bring, your heart to pierce.

Sweet she is, and like a diamond is her will,
And will a diamond be for you, dear John.
So love her, love her,
As she has been loved.
And she will love you
Now, forevermore.

March 2009

133

The Lord God In Embryo

"Mary? . . . Mary!"
The Angel said, pursuing.
"Did I catch you musing?
Hail, Mary. Do not be afraid,
I bring you news:
The Lord God of Hosts
Has chosen you –

"(Creator of the Sun and Moon
    and all the Stars!
Of angels, saints, and men,
And lovely maids like you.)

"In your case, full of grace –
There is no sin in you.
The Lord God has chosen you,
And asks you, Mary,
To bear His only Son,
The Redeemer of the world.

"Do not be afraid. Do not be ashamed.
Before Time was, He knew you, Mary,
And made you for this Holy Joy.
Blessed are you, Mary,
And blessed is His boy within you –

"Emmanuel,
Born of the House of David,

Brought to birth by you
For the saving of the world
(To bring all children home)."

"Yes," she said.

And the Spirit of the Lord
Poured Light in her,
The Father's seed
Took root
In Embryo.

Among all women, Mary,
He has chosen you.
Before Time was He chose you
And made you for this holy joy
Blessed are you, Mary!
And blessed in you is
His little boy.

For the Feast of the Annunciation, 2010

∞81∞

They Recognized Him in the Breaking of the Bread
For Hadley Arkes, on the day of his Baptism
April 24, 2010

We all have laughed with Hadley
We have admired him for years.
We love his civic reasoning
On law and natural right.

We love his love for Lincoln
And for Martin Luther King –
Who using natural law and right
Thrice made dear freedom ring!

I remember Judy telling me –
Oh! it was many years ago –
Hadley is already one of you,
But the time is not yet ripe.

This news that made me happy,
Made swim my ag-ed head.
 So I dared to say to Hadley,
"I miss you / at the breaking of the bread."

It seemed to me he believed like us
In God, in law, in love;
Even in the Word in Whom
All things come from above.

He hadn't quite met Jesus yet,
And needed time for that.
He read and thought and then – surprise! –
'Twas after all the *Church* that knocked him flat.

He met with Jesus through the Church
That bravely, bravely spoke the truth
Before the Courts, Planned Parenthood.
Media elites, and *New York Times* forsooth!

Dostoevsky, scholars say,
Read from the Gospels every day.
Come follow me, one day they say,
Come follow, come what may.

It takes a bit of trust, Lord knows,
Until a man is sure.
He has to try it out a while,
Confess, be rendered pure.

Part of the meal one has to eat
Includes a spoon of bitters,
Spinach and a bowl bitter p-p-porridge
In Hadley's case it took a lot of c-c-courage!

How will we know when Hadley's
Joined us, on Peter's barque, on board?
We'll recognize him breaking bread with us,
At the Table of the Lord.

As many grapes one wine do make
As many grains one bread
So one with us will Hadley be
At the Table of the Lord.

A unity with him much deeper
Than we ever knew before.
So shall we laugh, so shall we sing,
Tell jokes and drink once more.

But now our joy will ricochet
Through heavens' hosts and horde,
All the centuries will eat with us
At the Table of the Lord.

In the beginning only Jews did come
To the Table of the Lord.
So Hadley comes back home again
To the Table of His Lord.

Thank God for Hadley!
Thank God! All ye –
Greeks and Poles
And Englishmen,
Ye Ethiopes, and Jews,
Italians, and Frenchmen,
Ukrainians and *Rus* –

Ye Chinese, ye Japanese,
All ye from India and from the Philippines,
Ye Mexicans, Chileans,
And even Argentines –

Here, O Lord! comes everybody!
To the Table of the Lord,
Thank God! Comes *everybody*
To the Table of the Lord.

KAREN

Karen my love, my treasure, died in Washington, D.C., on August 12, 2009. Born in Minneapolis in 1937, brought up in Cresco, Iowa, taught printmaking by Mauricio Lasansky and painting by Oskar Kokoschka, Karen was teaching at Carleton College when we met, on a blind date, on March 26, 1962, the day that changed my life. It was a joy to be with her for forty-seven years. She deepened me in every way.

The Ballad of the Pilgrimage Primeval
While sailing in Alaskan Waters
August 30–September 5, 2009

Autumn war a cumin' in
When fifteen souls and Baby Christopher
Our Pilgrimage began
To time primeval, still, and dark,
Through marvels tall, and hidden coves and heights.
Through least known forests, among least known sights.

***

'Twas on St. Crispin's Day, September two,
The Lord's Year, two-thousand-nine,
When Earl Sin-Jims* Bowman death did cheat,
His duty, honor, courage to protect.
The others had gone on, and up and up, when he
His foot did cruelly twist; yet, hobbled, never once supine,
Pressed on up crevices, whose slippery mud
And stone-loose shale his bruis-ed ankle did torment.
Yet up he climbed, in pain, for others (he did think)
Depended on the sandwiches and drink
He bore deep ruck-sacked on his back.
So up he pressed, bypassed the lowest lake, up to the next,
And toward the tallest peak, his ankle groaned with pain.
Then hours after he turned down,
Sunset pressed in and evening's gown
Through bear-infested forest, ancient lichen, and under spell

---

* "Saint-James"

Of dripping trees, and moss, wet rocks and shifting footholds,
He stumbled as the darkness fell.

Poor Lady Karlyn on the *Michaela Rose* did fret
From two p.m. till eight. It was as if she knew her
Man had fallen hurt but honor-bound pressed on.
Reading she resumed, and conversation,
But always through the windows tried some motion, color, to
    espy.
When at last a rescue team was sent with torches
And–more important – GATORADE for all, good Lady Karlyn
Gaz-ed anxiously for torchlight to appear upon the hill
Beneath the ancient dark'ning canopy
"That's light!" she cried, and immediately
A blush suffused her countenance.

Sir Peter Wallison a man of honor was and soul,
Who recited the Ballad "Jean DuPrez" to us
As his father often had to him, and in his father's somber tones:
The earnestness of Jean, the pathos of the little boy,
Who preferred to give his own life more than shoot a hero-
    friend –
So shot the evil Major dead.

And so Sir Peter took a fall for me, when on a slippery
Footbridge he tried to break a staff
By kicking on a too-long slimy branch. Alas!
His heavy boot did slide upon the wet and slippery wood
And down pulled Peter from the bridge – a thud upon his ribs.
The branch he broke. And very near his ribs.
From there I walked, stout staff in hand –
But Peter's hand, upon his aching ribs.

Frieda looked with disapproval on this honorable deed.
"I love your sense of honor, Peter,

But, please, protect your ribs. I hate to
Bandage and to bathe you just when all
My friends and I are busy bringing down
Obamacare. It won't be good for you, my dear."
Frieda, it may be, was the brightest 'mongst us guests,
And witty was, and kind. And practical.

The Earl of Casenovia, Sir Karl Z., is married
To the lovely Princess, Ann, and yet along Alaskan paths he
    tarried,
Taking photo after photo (but not of lovely Ann) of mushrooms –
Tall and squat, and grey and brown and red, even ugliest of
    blooms.
He then produc-ed instant photo slides of our whole
Pilgrimage
All set to Brahms. In whose achievement lay a German
    discipline.
His lovely Ann doth walk with him along the way
Of Methodism. That's the adverbial religion, which modifies
    the world –
Stresses common ground, and counsels: "Sweetly, kindly,
    modestly,
Temperately, and gently" – so goeth they
For miles, yet with an appetite for vigorous sports
And quiet smiles.

Sir John McClaughry was the pillar of our team, a knight of
    vast experiences,
Of wars too numerous to count, and wounds and scars to show.
And tales and stories long and short, and blow by blow.
He is of vigor bountiful, and generous to a fault. And modest,
    too.
He told more jokes at his expense than any in our crew.
Sir John, like no Britisher since Agincourt, hath deep, deep

Love for Frogs. He battles mightily 'gainst their discrimination.
"Fair Play for Frogs!" he shouts. "The Principles of Eton we
    must keep!
Killing frogs is an abomination,
Unworthy of this noble Isle."
His hero is Sir Nestle Frobish, of whom he speaks with loving
    guile.

His dear, dear wife, another Lady Ann, than whom no kinder
    soul
Was ever known. She let me talk about myself,
And talk and talk and talk.
In an heroic effort to restore my sanity,
Her capacity for listening was endless as my vanity.
Cheery, too, is she, with strength and manner whole.
And also she does knit, with patience and with zip.
While no one looked, she kissed Sir Nestle Frobish on the lip.

Christina Sommers might have been a lady of the stage
With clear-toned voice for singing, and tonier French,
She longs to play Commedienne Française.
Lifting graceful fingers through her hair
And laughing in the glory of the sun,
She dances for the fun,
And, like our Mr. Coyne prepares
A three-star bouillabaisse.

Kim Dennis plays the lonely libertarian
Who (she says) community be always hating,
Unless she has chosen it, it is too suffocating.
Put her on a trail with seven others –
Up ahead she'll spring until she is alone.
When twelve are gathered in the lounge,
Out kayaking she goes, without her phone.

Yet in our company her eyes were merriest.
Yes, in teasing as she danced she was the merriest.

No mortal eyes have ever seen two parents
Youthful, just sixteen months a-nurturing their first,
Who mother-father are with lighter touch,
And happy are, and joyous with their child.
They also awe the older folks with their wild
Passion for all hikes, and skis, and water sports,
With Christopher the Third on back, when walking in the wood
To swirling pools where black bears 'n grizzlies come to fish.
A lucky couple are those two – (pardon me) those three.
And lucky also we,
Who sailed with them.

Now of Ayaán I sing. Incandescent, fearless conscience.
Spirit, laughter in her eyes, courageous, quick of wit
And intelligence and logic, diplomatic skills,
Political experience. This lover of "a-MER-i-ca!"
With boundless energy did run with Kim.
She is no early riser, though:
Why should she be? She has already lived three lives
Where most of us live one.

Sometimes I fear for her.
I wish she were my daughter
So I could hold her tight
And tell her of the pride I have in her.
And how God loves her.

About our host, Sir Christopher: Sir Christopher DeMuth
Is peerless in his courtesie, his consideration,
Gentle manners and intelligence. Loyal he is, and kind.
His laugh is as great as echoes in an isolated vale,

Taste he has – to tell a tale –
A marvelous taste in friends.
We thank him for inviting us.
We thank him for including us
Among his lucky friends.

***

In our week's Pilgrimage all-backwards to primeval time
Where we heard bits of glaciers fall,
And ancient lichen saw on ancient trees,
Where bears kill salmon by biting off their heads,
Bald Eagles soar in circles, gimlet-eyed and swift.
The King of all sea lions swims up from the boiling waters,
Heaving heavy blubber up, up on the reddish rocks,
Raised up his head above the rest,
Two hundred prostrate
Serfs, and gurgled out a glorious roar.

There Christopher our voyage led
About which we shall often dream when we are old abed.

***

When I came on this cruise, it must be said,
I was a pretty empty man. I didn't really want to talk.
I still could laugh, but that felt wrong.
I really wanted just to sit alone and let the pain wash in.
Instead my friends, the warmth of your own hearts
Brought me back into the light.
I thank you, friends, for giving back my sight.

***

To claim that this is poetry would truly be perverse.
One wishes that at least, my friends, it cudda bin – well –
     verse. [The End]

September 5, 2009

146

ೞ83ಏ

For Karen, On Christmas orn 2009
After Mass

Full of grace!
Full of grace.
Full of grace...!

Mother, who this day
brought us Our Love
and our Redeemer
Take into your care a mother like yourself,
Our much loved, so-loved Karen.
Honor her for her self-sacrifice
Who gave her life for us
And especially for me
She gave up too much art
So dear to her for mine
She did not count on dying first
But left so much she longed to do unfinished.

Please embrace her and comfort her
And speak to her with love
Remind her of her words of you
As she watched "The Passion,"
Scrubbing harder with her tears
The dearest blood of your dear Son.
And how she loved your "Magnificat."

Please, Good Lady, Mother,
Speak to her with tender love

147

As for ages you have been known to do,
Take her by the hand to those she loves,
John Paul the Second, Father Richard,
Irving, Bill, Clare, Avery and Eunice,
And, God willing that he's there,
Oskar Kokoschka, who called her
"My little darling Karen," and singled out
Her talent and her promise for all to hear.

Take her, too, to all the others whom she loved.
Sts. Thomas, Teresa, John o' the Cross,
And John of the Apocalypse,
T.S. Eliot, Rilke, Dostoevsky,
And all of those with whom she long communed.
Take her around, dear Mother, honor
Her self-sacrifice.

If Heaven is a conversation, dearest Hostess,
Take her kindly where she will be happiest –
For her, that is, where can learn the most.
Shepherd her, protect her,
But do not think she is too shy –
Give her your smile and let her go her way.

December 25, 2009

Composed at the Immaculate Conception Cathedral, Denver,
Colorado.

⋙84⋘

On Loving Karen

Thank you, lady, for reminding me what it was like
To fall in love with Karen
Fifty years ago.
It was her eyes that did me in,
Blue as the sapphire stones
She bought along the Indian Ocean.
Blue, with sadness deep behind them,
And merriment like candle's flames on golden foil.

Eyes incapable of malice,
Radiant from her heart.
We talked and talked, newly met,
Though we had known
Each other ever since forever.

We knew the darkness and the night –
That may have been our deepest bond.
We weren't afraid of night.
A woman who has suffered much, as Tolstoi wrote,
Inflames a lover's heart.

I cannot say if Karen loved me.
That was a word she rationed,
As if in uttering it she lost her self –
Which fighting to hold safe so many years,
Impressionable and unconflictive
(As she wished to be) she could not give away.

To say would utterly destroy her, *poof*!
Like dust she'd blow away.
No, it was crucial that she act with love
But seldom say the word.
Crucial that she trust.
Crucial to stay the Self
She had, so much embattled, won.

But oh! I loved her
And loving her burst into joy,
An oven suddenly ignited.

Who could not love her shyness,
Her evasive smile of pleasure.
Her self-dramatizing humor about herself?
Her idle dream had been to be an actress
A comedienne of dance and music,
Light of heart and blithe.
What she really wanted
Was to be the next Picasso.
Kokoschka had told her that she could.

She was self-mockingly insistent
That her I married, for her mind,
To which I readily agreed
Although not wholly true. Yes,
Without her darkness of experience,
Without her wit,
Without her flashes to the heart of things,
My soul could not have been so deeply wounded.
But I was stricken also by her figure
And her shy, shy smile.

Still later, then, her works of art I saw,

Which took my breath away.
A woman always struggling,
Always suffering,
Conflicted, active, bold.
Uncompromisingly,
She stripped away the skin from straining sinews
And showed live bones in pain
(Or maybe only tension)
And underneath each face the mask of death.
She saw life truly
In its awfulness and joy.

Fiercest angels did she wrestle.
"Every angel," her Rilke wrote, "is terrible."

———

Parting (in 1962), I handed her my novel,
About a soul stripped down to nothingness
Yet rejoicing in the dark
(Where alone God can be found).
Her favorite books were Avila's,
And The Dark Night of the Soul.
Mine, too.

She thought I'd been pretentious,
She later wrote,
For handing her my book.
But she read it on her journey home
One end to the other.
She slyly hinted that she liked it.

So we were free to love like children
Who had learned to trust,
Yet knew the fingers on the windowpane,

In darkness and in rain.
We were made to meet.
Or so I felt in thirty minutes
Across the booth from her in Harvard Square.

Most extraordinary thing:
I had described her in my novel
Two years before we met.
Lovely girl, an artist,
Upon Bernini's bridge at midnight
When the Tiber turned to silver
Beneath a silver moon.*

So I knew that I had known her
And would marry her.
Knew, but didn't say a word.
For four days we did nothing
But go out together.
She was fearless driving Boston streets.
That was what convinced me
She was tough.
More tough than I.
Which was in my dream.

I knew I loved her, almost *bam*!
It took her longer:
Three close suitors in hot pursuit,
Each one aspiring lawyer as if
In answer to her lawyer father's prayers.
One did love her mightily, I later learned.
Thank God she took a leap toward me.

---

* I here compress the actual plot.

We were apart all summer,
She at the Worcester Craft School,
And I in Europe, steadily describing to her
All I saw, and quietly insinuating...
We were meant to meet.
A hundred letters sent in all–
Desperate to hold her heart.

Just last month,
My sister found her photo,
Sitting on my parents' lawn
In September, 1962.
My brother Dick (whom K. had met at Harvard)
Was on his way to Bangladesh,
And Karen planned her drive from Iowa
To pick me up, both Harvard-bound,
To bid dear Dick farewell
(Little did we know it was forever).

She sits upon the lawn her knees drawn up
In short black shorts, a Vee-striped blouse
Of orange and brown, and on her head
A turban striped the same.
A skinny, gawky kid in shell-rimmed glasses
Sits as close to her as decency permits.
Can that be me?
Even then I asked myself,
Can this be me?
How can that fellow sit with such a one
In total inner peace?

Our honeymoon some ten months thence,
On Minnesota's Forest Lake–
My beloved walked into the bath,

A towel on arm but not a stitch of clothes,
And closed the door.
Let out a piercing shriek, fell back,
Slid downward noisily onto the floor.
Had burglers broken in?

Leaping to the door, I saw a bat attacking her.
I pulled her out, and stepped inside
To face the bat, and illumination struck my mind:
"So this is what a married man is for?"
Gulping folded up a towel to swing
And watched its swoops
As closely as a pitcher's wicked curve
When it buzzed in and dove at me.
I caught it fairly, brought it down
But in the motion felled myself.

Here Karen showed her wit,
Broke in, a basket in her hands
Which she slapped down upon the now-dazed bat.
"How do we get it out of here?"
I asked with weak male reason.
She answered me with motion,
Returning with a cardboard square
To slip beneath the basket.
Cool as a cop she marched it to the darkened door
And flicked it up into the night.
What a cool, cool girl, I marvel,
Then and now.

She also showed me what a coward I could be
When once at dinner little three-year-old
Began to choke, in desperation turning red.
I froze. Not K. She leapt across the kitchen

Plunged her finger down the throat,
Pulled out the villainous blob.
Not the first or only time
She moved with wit and bravery
While I sat panicked, turning pale.

———

St. Thomas (Aquinas) wrote,
"Of all friendships,
Marriage is by far the greatest."
I used to tell my classes that,
And say that it is true.
The only thing – I used to warn – is this:
If you don't like the truth about yourself,
Then don't get married.
When you live close in,
Illusions are expensive.
So once the honeymoon is over,
Your lover's duty is
To puncture every one of yours –
One by painful one.
My lover pricked an awful lot of mine.
Especially my conceits.

Annoying faults my lover also had,
So I did edit them, much to her pain.
She had a low opinion of herself,
So one more fault was more than she could bear.
I added to her pain. I'm sorry that I did.

Oh, Glory! I loved Karen,
Love her still. Irradiant soul.
Valiant, courageous, strong,
Yet soft and vulnerable.

Beautiful with full and loving sensual beauty.
Funny, amusing, telling tales about herself –
Confessing all her silly faults
Before I found them out.

She was wonderful to hug.
She loved to hug.
She needed many hugs –
Or maybe I did.

And now she seems so close to me.
I commune with her incessantly
Since now she sees me even to my inner self.
I hear her laughing quite a lot
As I go bouncing light to light
And wall to wall, a pinball
In a slanted box. She enjoys
My blunders. Always has.

It seems she has told everyone
(Before she died) I worried her –
"He doesn't know a thing around the house.
He cannot do it for himself."
It isn't true, of course. I do okay.
But in an obvious sense, b'god,
The girl was right.

There is no other like her. She is unique.
I was lucky, lucky, lucky,
To be with her nearly fifty years.
That is why I look at photos,
Read old letters, and let the burning
Burn my soul.

February 14, 2010